For Jago & Harvey, never stop exploring.

This book was made, printed and bound in Cornwall using paper from responsibly managed forests.

Cornwall
An Alphabetical Adventure

Written by
Ben Rowswell

Illustrated by
Amelia Brooks

Kernow a'gas dynergh!

Welcome to Cornwall, come and explore,
the South West peninsula that we adore.
We'll show you some sights, and a few hidden gems,
there's room to bring your family and friends.

Waste no more time... turn the page and let's enter...

...drive down the A30 right through the centre.

Booby's Bay
St Ives
Minions
Perranporth
Idless Woods
Looe
Skinners Bottom
Godrevy Lighthouse
Land's End
St Michael's Mount
Mousehole
Falmouth

A30
Look out the window, the green land is hilly.
The peak to the North is known as Brown Willy.
Devon
Cornwall
Brown Willy
At 1,378 feet (420m)
above sea level Brown Willy
is Cornwall's highest peak.

C is for Chough, who sits on the crest,
red feet and beak, with black on its chest.

Do it Dreckly (that's anytime soon),
right after breakfast or nearer to noon.

There's no need to rush, it won't be too long,
sit while you wait and whistle a song.

Visit the Eden Project now and again,
to learn about plants and gaze at the glen.
Listen to music, ice skate or zip wire,
each year the redwoods grow higher and higher.

Giant redwoods have been planted along the entrance to the Eden Project.

Learn to paint Fishing boats down in the ports,
like Falmouth or Fowey, and buy fish of all sorts.
Bream, gurnard, haddock and hake,
scallops and mackerel look good on a plate.

Cornwall is great for a walk or a strut;
can you smell the sweet coconut?
The scent is from the yellow flowers of Gorse,
a spiky tough shrub that grows wild on the moors.

H is for Heartlands, an old mining patch;
where tin was once a hell of a catch.
The world's greatest miners tackled these hills,
then travelled the world to use their fine skills.

It's also for hogs pudding,
cut and grilled sausage rings,
a Cornish tradition, a breakfast of kings!

In summer the shops all tout their Ice Creams,
with flavours that you can imagine in dreams.
Rocky road, toffee crisp, cinnamon crunch...
Can I have one please? I've eaten my lunch!

The J is for Jam, to put on your scone.
Eat them all up they won't last too long.
Finish it off in Cornish tradition,
a dollop of cream in the perfect position.

The Cornish method is to spread with strawberry jam, and finally top with a spoonful of clotted cream.

Kynance Cove...
a picturesque scene;
a beach and a river,
and grass that is green.
So many tourists have
walked on the sand,
including a prince and
the queen of the land.

The cove became popular in the early Victorian era, with many distinguished visitors including Queen Victoria and Prince Albert, and the poet Alfred Tennyson.

In summer the Lifeguards patrol between flags,
with longboards and boats and first aid in bags.
Running and swimming, the beach is their gym,
keeping an eye while you go for a swim.

Red and yellow flags indicate a supervised swim zone.
The black and white flags are for surf craft.
The red flag means don't enter the water.

Mount Hawke has a skate park great for new tricks,
ride on the halfpipe and do some cool flips.
Chat to some friends and test the hot cooking,
dad has a skate when he thinks you're not looking.

Towan

Tolcarne

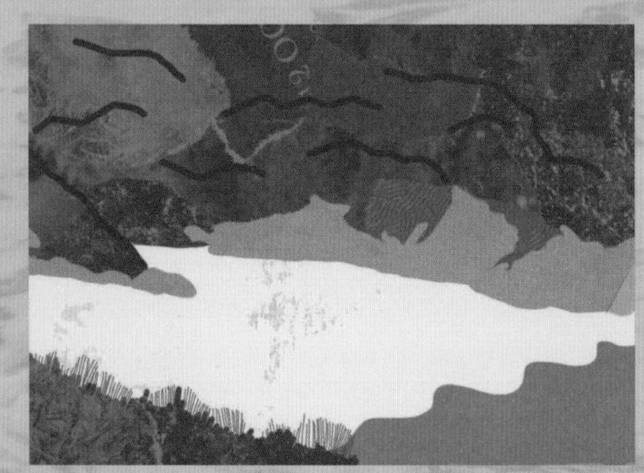
Great Western

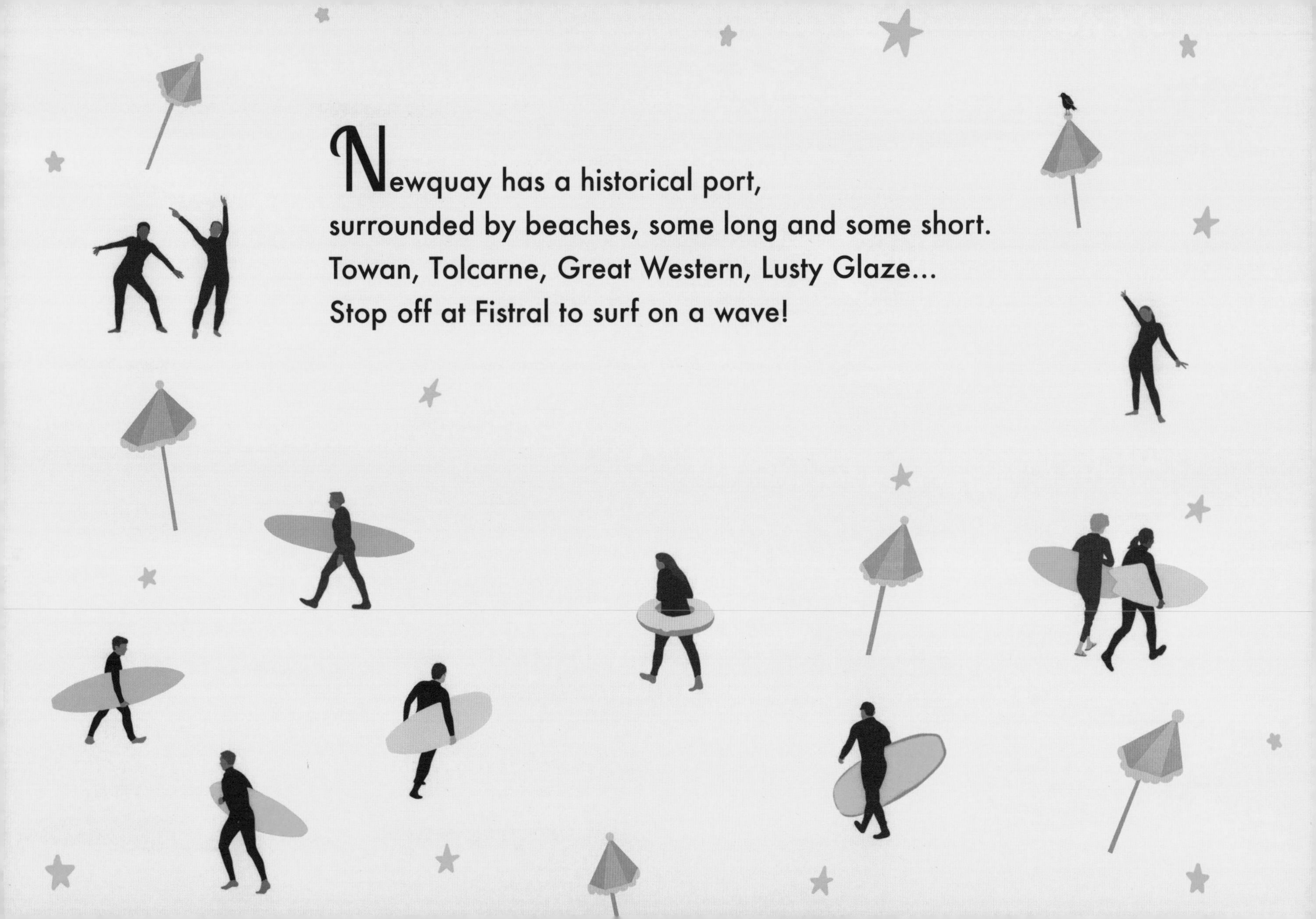

Newquay has a historical port,
surrounded by beaches, some long and some short.
Towan, Tolcarne, Great Western, Lusty Glaze...
Stop off at Fistral to surf on a wave!

O is for **O**rchards, full of plump apples.
Sit under a tree where the sun is all dappled.
Pick them and eat them, or squeeze out the juice.
Try some cold cider and have a quick snooze.

Onion Redstreak, Pascoe's Pippin, Pignose, Queenie or a sweet Merlin are all varieties of Cornish apple.

P for potatoes, pepper and pastry.
Along with the rest to make a great Pasty!
Buy and eat hot from your favourite shop,
or ask gran for her recipe... now that can't
be topped!

A Quoit is a structure that makes you consider,
whether these stones were moved with a digger!
Did they use magic? Did they use strength?
Or were they moved with a special wavelength?

The Royal Cornwall Show is an annual event,
with animals, diggers and beers in a tent.
But Rugby's our game and it's followed with passion,
on match day black and gold is the fashion.

Don't feed the Seagulls says the sign on the stand.
Hey! Come back, he took it right out my hand!
They're crafty and strong and have stickers for eyes;
and will tear out the bins when they're searching for pies.

The Tamar, the TATE, Tintagel or Truro?
Torpoint, Trevone, Tresillian or Temple?
So many towns beginning with T...
Let's stop at Tregothnan for a nice cup of Tea!

Tregothnan estate has been growing and supplying Britain's first home-grown tea since 2005.

Underground tunnels go down through the rocks,
for miles men dug and they heard the strange knocks.

Down through the ground and under the sea,
hearing waves crash that they couldn't see.

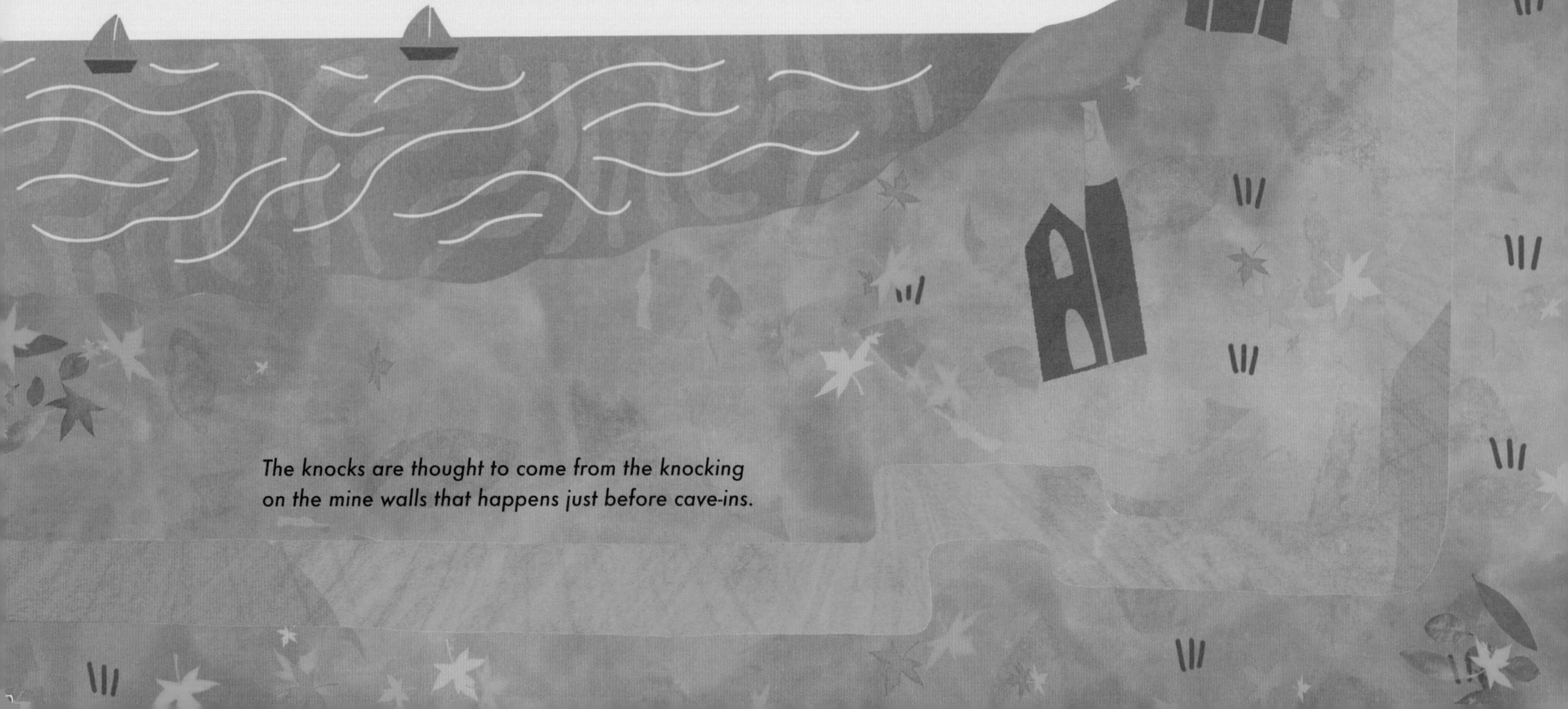

The knocks are thought to come from the knocking on the mine walls that happens just before cave-ins.

Not many places begin with a V.
But here are two you surely must see:
Ventongimps with its bog, ponds and spring;
full of dragonflies, and wild birds that sing.
Veryan's roundhouses with thatched roofs are quaint
and nearby a burial site of a saint.

Considered to be the largest Bronze-Age burial mound in England the Cornish saint, King Gerennius (Geraint) is said to be buried here. Local folklore suggests that the burial mound contains a golden boat with silver oars, on which his body was brought across Gerrans Bay.

Wellies are a must
for half of the year, for
walking in forests with
badgers and deer.

Walk the long coastpath
but watch you have grip,
as some of it's steep
and you won't want to slip!

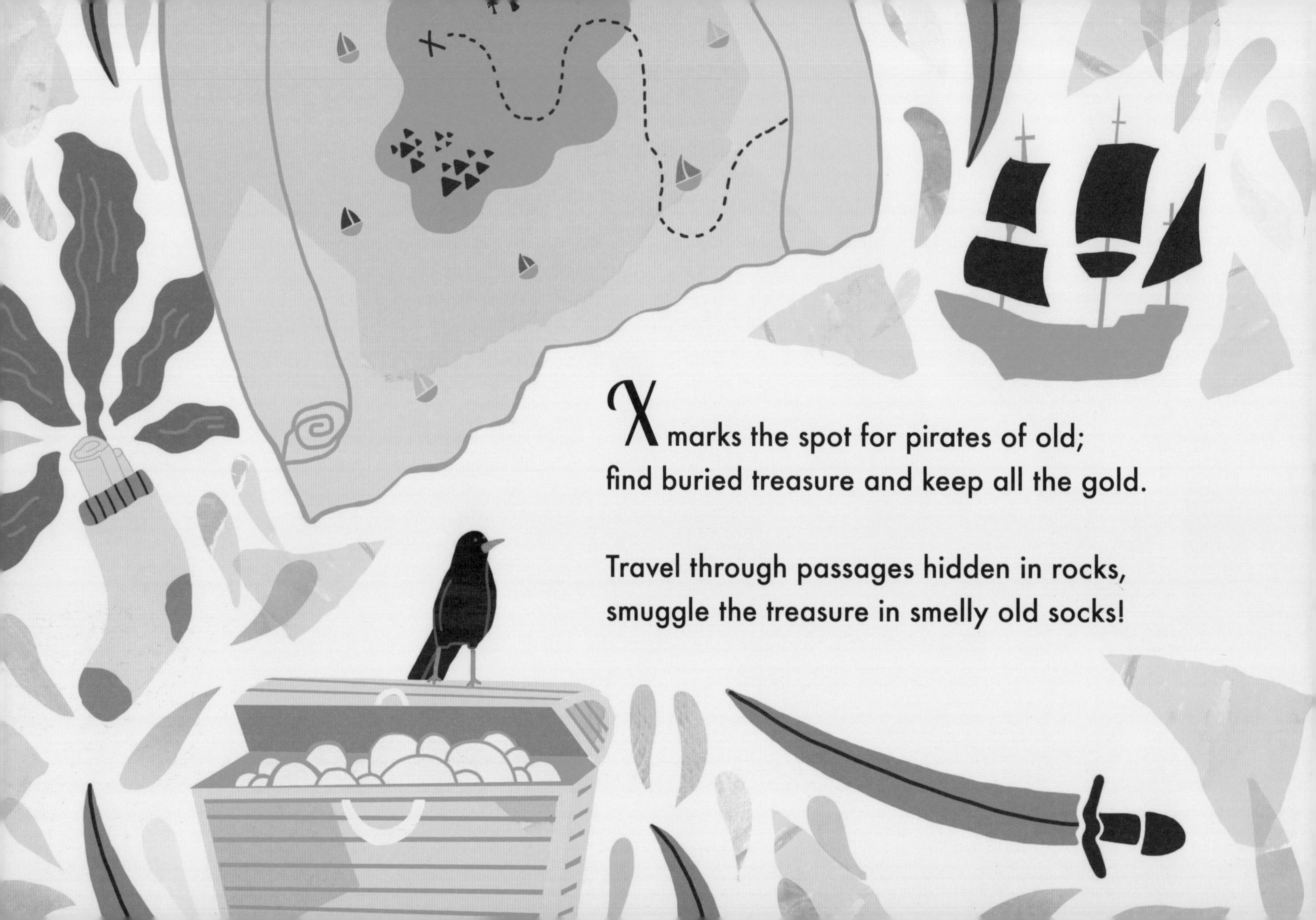

X marks the spot for pirates of old;
find buried treasure and keep all the gold.

Travel through passages hidden in rocks,
smuggle the treasure in smelly old socks!

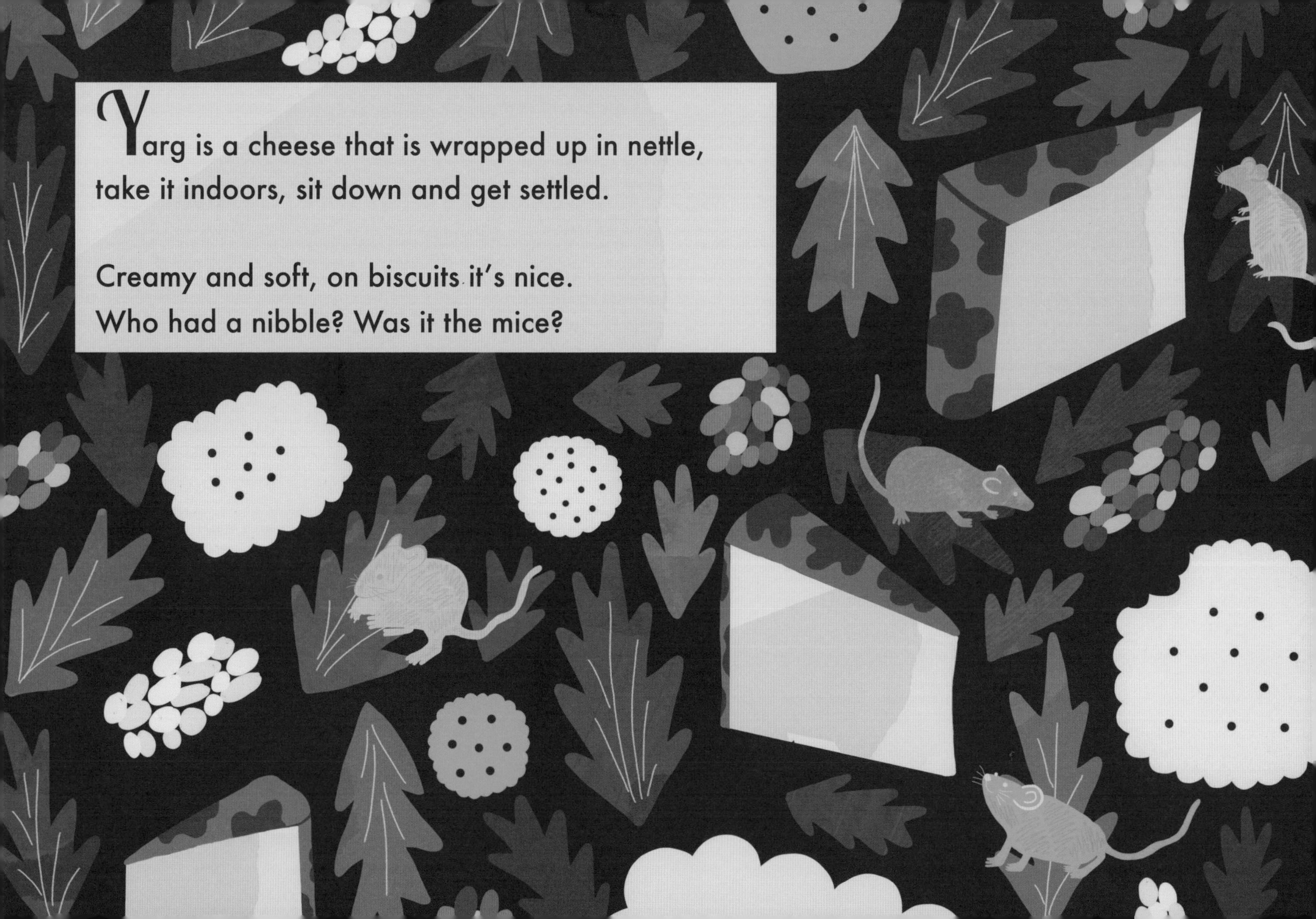

Yarg is a cheese that is wrapped up in nettle,
take it indoors, sit down and get settled.

Creamy and soft, on biscuits it's nice.
Who had a nibble? Was it the mice?

The last place to visit on this special tour,

is Zennor, a village all rugged and raw.
Search for the mermaid with mirror and comb,
stay here a while but don't stay alone.

Because if she hears you singing a song,
she'll show you her tail and tempt you along.
Under the water among all the fishes,
granting you all of your favourite wishes.

Before the book closes, promise me this.
Close your eyes and make one final wish,
say it aloud and make it come true.
Explore Cornwall again, come back very soon!

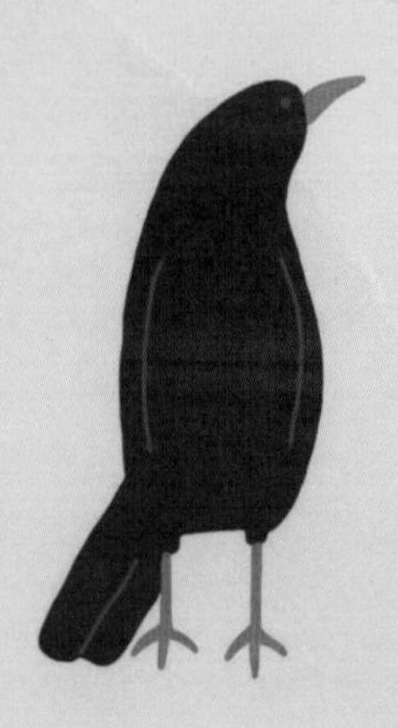